Volcano Dancing

Owen O'Neill

To Sally
Thanks for walking
miles to the cash point
Best
Owen
x

THIRSTY BOOKS
EDINBURGH

First published 2003
Thirsty Books
an imprint of
Argyll Publishing
Glendaruel
Argyll PA22 3AE
Scotland
www.argyllpublishing.co.uk

**British Library Cataloguing-in-Publication Data.
A catalogue record for this book is available from the British Library.**

ISBN 9781906134808

Cover Photo
Michael Thorsnes

Printing
Bell & Bain Ltd, Glasgow

Owen O'Neill's people were flax scutchers
and barbers who shaved with cut-throat razors
sharpened on leather belts.
Some chewed War Horse tobacco,
spat long distances
and threw tin buckets at Orange flute bands.
Owen's mother give birth to sixteen children
and was never beaten at hopscotch.
His father would sometimes black-up, dress as a Sikh
and sell shirts round the neighbourhood.
His aunt once ate her Christmas dinner out of a big
glass ashtray and commented how the indents were
perfect to rest her knife and fork.
Owen would like to thank all the members
of his very large family, living and dead,
for their flights of dangerous, dark alcoholic,
deep-rooted madness and instability,
without which he would not have a story to tell.

CONTENTS

Man in the Queue

The man behind me in the queue for the cinema
spoke in my dead father's voice. A heart jolting
moment, that made me want to turn around, but I didn't
because I wanted to listen to my Dad a while longer.

That deep soft lilt of County Tyrone, those same flat
vowels, with little nervous coughs in between, as he
talked about the tragedy in New York. 'Ah jaysus now
they musta suffered them people, aye, God help them, aye.'

Gentle intakes of breath to punctuate the silence of
saying nothing. He talked about the 'moratur flyin
and the confewshun and the awful dust and the Feyer
Breegade and the men an weemin screemin, sure

Jaysus it wud brack yer heart ta luck at it. Aye, a tarrable
day, tarrable day indeed.' I nodded and smiled to myself,
tears lumped in my throat, for I knew that this is exactly
what my father would have said.

There was silence for a moment, and I wanted the
man to say something else. Something like, 'I'm sorry
son, sorry about the drinkin and neglectin ye all them years,
and batein yer muther and all that arguin and fightin

ah know ah wasn't a good father. I was a selfish bad
tempered drunken hoor. But ah did love ye. I was a fool.
And then not ticking care of meself, dying on ye at fifty-five.
Sure that was a bad carryon son, that was fucking stupid.'

You'll Never Get Another Job Like That

And what kept you? Some little fucker was
always saying to me as I grew, what kept you?
And I knew it was sarcasm that deserved
at best a shrug. Even at that age
I was no mug.

And then, when I had grown, some silly bastard
was always looking at his watch and saying,
what time do you call this eh? And I knew
it was unanswerable dialogue that deserved
at best a shrug.

So I'd say
Stick your fucking poxy shit bollox of a job
up your ass you wee tight-arsed bigoted
bowler-hatted bandy-legged fuckwit!

I'm self-employed now.

Judas

Judas. Kissed and never said a word.
A kiss was enough.
His kiss of death.
The kiss that killed him.

Judas. What a chance you took.
Jesus took no chances.
Jesus knew all along.
He should have warned you Judas.

Jesus should have warned you.
That Jesus.
What a Judas
he turned out to be.

Long Grass Falling

The desperate tribal chant of the Rosary ranted
around his lovely head, cold to the touch. All I
could think of was his freckled forehead, beaded with sweat in
the middle of my young summer when he'd stripped to the waist to
mow the back field.

Long, graceful, strokes of the scythe
laying the grass low, and more alive, than I ever
knew grass could be. Suddenly,
the praying stopped. But still my grief refused to
move, it lay stunned, like a road accident.

Then I was back in the field, behind that curved
lethal blade, he let me hold the wooden handles
made me unafraid, his large hands wrapped gently
over mine, we moved together as one, and the grass
fell slowly into line, to the sun.

I carried his coffin. A tremendous weight ached all the
way through me. I tried to imagine him, stiff and
silent, closed in from the light, his large hands beaded
and wrapped together. But I couldn't. I could only see
the scythe and the long grass falling.

Shouting from the Scaffold

Extract from the award winning one-man play 'Shouting from the Scaffold' (Edinburgh 1996)

THE YEAR IS 1974. OWEN IS EIGHTEEN YEARS OLD AND HAS BEEN OFFERED A JOB ON THE OIL PIPELINE IN SCOTLAND.

OWEN: The job in Germany didn't come off but I've been offered a job in Scotland on the oil pipeline. Three hundred a week. The train tickets came this morning along with a slip of paper with MEET AT THE GREEN TEA HUT GLASGOW CENTRAL MON JUNE 6TH AT 2.15. So bonnie Scotland here I come!

MUSIC CUE: SCOTTISH DANCE BAND.

OWEN: Ecclefechan! That's where I ended up. The green tea hut at Glasgow Central was unmissable. It was a big green shed with TEA HUT written across the roof in giant white letters. There was about forty other men there with slips of paper in their hands with MEET AT THE GREEN TEA HUT written on them. Then this big ugly bastard with piggy eyes and a head like a weasel appeared carrying a clipboard. He began to shout out names. Adams Paddy! Burns Tommy! Clancy Michael! Donovan Liam! And all these guys were jumping from the queue, hands up, smiling, like they'd won the Sweepstake. They were given a piece of paper with a van registration number on it and then they were told to go to the car park, find the van and be driven to their location. My name was the last to be called. O'Neill Owen! I stepped forward. Weasel Head's piggy eyes ran me up and down. He had a disgusted look on his face. He gazed over the top of my head into the crowd of commuters and shouted loudly at no one in particular. O'Neill Owen! 'That's me I said. 'I'm O'Neill Owen'. It sounded weird saying my name back to front like that and I almost laughed. Weasel Head studied my application form very closely, occasionally glancing at me with contempt. What he saw was a skinny eighteen year old who looked fifteen, with shoulder length red hair, wearing a Led Zeppelin tee shirt, torn jeans and plimsoles, carrying a small battered leather suitcase with a belt strapped around the middle of it. He handed me my piece of paper.

WEASEL HEAD: You look like my fuckin niece!

OWEN: There were about fifty identical white vans in the car park. It took me half an hour to find mine. The driver was a grumpy bastard called Ford and he was a dead ringer for Frank Zappa.

FORD: Bout fuckin time an all get in!

OWEN: Where am I going?

FORD: Ecclefechan!

OWEN: I was none the wiser. I thought he was swearing at me. The journey took two hours and it was horrible. I tried to make conversation but everyone ignored me and talked amongst themselves. There was this one man, older than the rest, possibly in his fifties, staring quietly out of the back window. I remembered his name was Clancy. It was the expression on his face that made me feel really depressed. He looked washed out and tired of life and then suddenly, as if he had read my mind and without looking up he said softly. 'Don't worry son it's going to be all right.' I thanked him and struck up a conversation asking him where he was from in

Ireland and was he looking forward to the new job and did he know where we were going? But he just kept staring out of the back window and then he said it again, softer this time. 'Don't worry son It's going to be all right'. That's when I realised he was talking to himself.

OWEN: It was after midnight by the time we reached Ecclefechan. There was one hotel in Ecclefechan the Ecclefechan Hotel and they didn't have enough rooms available for eight men. They weren't expecting us until the following day. So we were asked if we minded sharing a bed just for one night. After much embarrassed laughter and predictable jokes about Vaseline and who was going to sleep with the little ginger one, the beds were sorted out and I was left to share with Clancy who still hadn't spoken a word to anyone. The manager handed Clancy the room keys. Clancy took them and then opened his little holdall and took out something wrapped in brown paper. He opened it up and showed the manager six big beef sausages. The manager stared at them and Clancy said:

CLANCY: Could you cook these for me?

MANAGER: Cook them?

CLANCY: Aye. Fry them up for me.

MANAGER: I'm sorry sir the kitchens are closed now and all the Chefs have gone home and we don't cook food privately for guests.

OWEN: Clancy held the sausages closer to the managers face.

CLANCY: My wife made these sausages. She made them special like. For me. They have to be cooked soon or they'll go bad.

MANAGER: I'm very sorry sir but as I said the kitchen is closed. . . . if you're hungry there might be some sandwiches left in the bar.

OWEN: Clancy stared long and hard at the manager and then in a very soft voice said. . .

CLANCY: You don't want to know. . . how special these sausages are. . . because your spontaneity and generosity of spirit have been crushed. I pity you.

OWEN: Clancy flung the sausages back into his hold-all and stormed off up the stairs with me close behind him.

PAUSE.

OWEN: I was relieved when I saw the size of the bed. It was enormous. Clancy went over and sat by the window cradling the hold-all in his arms like a baby. I tried several times to engage him in conversation but eventually gave up, brushed my teeth, got undressed and crawled into bed. I tried my best to get to sleep but it's very difficult to sleep when you have a mute sausage freak in your bedroom staring out of the window with a hold-all in his arms. I was just about to drop off when I heard him getting undressed. He got into the bed very quietly. I thought I could hear him whispering but I couldn't be sure. Then he laid back on the headboard and I was just beginning to doze off again when I heard a slurping sound, slurping and soft chomping like he was having trouble removing his false teeth. It went on and on this slurping, so I turned around to say something and I just could not believe my eyes. . . Clancy was eating his wife's special sausages. Big tears rolled quietly down his long sad face. He put his forefinger and thumb gently to his lips and pulled out the sausage skin completely unbroken and dropped it on the floor beside the bed. He ate all six sausages.

PAUSE.

OWEN: The next morning my nervous system was shattered by a jumbo jet taking off in the room. A little woman in a head-scarf pulled the plug on her big Hoover and the noise stopped. Clancy was kneeling by the side of the bed fully dressed with two hands clasped to his face praying. Then suddenly the woman was screeching at the top of her voice 'Am no hoovering that up ye ken!' Clancy ignored her, blessed himself and left. 'Disgusting bloody filthy bastards ye'll rot in hell.' She slammed the door nearly off its hinges. It was half six and I was late so I leapt out of bed and straight into my working gear. On my way out I noticed the six sausage skins lying in a pile on Clancy's side of the bed.

PAUSE.

OWEN: If we hadn't been held up by a sheep jam, I would've missed the van. I've never seen as many sheep in one place in all my life. Hundreds of them milling around, no dog or shepherd in sight just sheep and Weasel Head stuck in the middle of them, steam coming out of his ears trying to kick them off the road.

WEASEL HEAD: Come on! Shoosh! Ya bastards! Fuck off out of it! Does anybody know who owns these fuckin sheep?

OWEN: Weasel Head caught me smirking and came straight for me.

WEASEL HEAD: And you can wipe that fuckin smile off your face! When we get to the hill I want you to start filling hundredweight bags with sand. You'll fill two hundred bags a day and if you fall below that target you can fuck off to whatever doss hole you crawled out of!

OWEN: Weasel Head then caught sight of Clancy, who was sitting on the side of the road staring into the sky.

WEASEL HEAD: What's that cunt doing?

OWEN: He stormed over to Clancy falling over sheep.

WEASEL HEAD: Get into the fuckin van you ponce. I'm not paying you to look at clouds!

OWEN: Clancy completely ignored Weasel Head, got up and walked over to me.

CLANCY: I'm sorry young fellah. I had to eat them you see. She made them specially and. . . well. . . she hasn't got long you know, it's now in her lungs. . . only a matter of time. She didn't want me there to see her like that. . . but I'm going home to be with her. Sorry I kept you awake.

WEASEL HEAD: When you two queers are fuckin ready we'll go!

OWEN: And then Clancy did something so extraordinary that I will never forget it as long as I live. He went up to Weasel Head. . . and started to sing. . . He had the most beautiful voice.

CLANCY: (SINGING)
How sweet is the rose by yon bonny blue stream,
where the curlews do call though it's part of a dream.

OWEN: Weasel Head didn't know quite what was happening. He took two steps back and I'm sure it was fear that I saw in his eyes.

WEASEL HEAD: Get in the fucking van you mad cunt! Or you're down the road!

OWEN: Clancy carried on singing. Raising the song to a new level and then he suddenly grabbed me and started to waltz me around the road. The rage on Weasel Head's face made me dance like I've never danced before. The men in the van stared at us, their mouths hanging open.

CLANCY: You're a young lad. You don't have to work for a scumbag like him. Life is too short.

OWEN: The van roared off over the fields with Weasel Head screaming and foaming at the mouth. Clancy sang the rest of the song and we danced on watched by five hundred sheep.

First Love

No light, taut.
Me and another
framed in the dark.
She taught me
in the pictures.

The light came on.
Oh the light!
But she was gone
and so were my
Dolly Mixtures!

It Was Only Eleven o' Clock

Found him lying on the broad
of his back.
Inside the ring he had made
for himself.

He had always told me that he'd
been born with extra skin on
his skull. Said it was his lucky
cap. I believed him.

The sky was in his eyes. My shame was,
it was too early for this.
Where was the night that protected
such people.

Come on get up. You can't lie here.
It's the middle of the day. For Christ's sake
Get up. Come on! Stop making a show of
Yourself. Get up!

Away you and enjoy yourself son. I'm
all right here, look at that Cumulus Stratus,
my favourite. You wouldn't see that if you were
walking about.
There's change in me jacket, take it
take it all, go to the dance tonight.

So I did. Some who knew, watched and
understood, smiled even. Then there were
those who saw a young man robbing a drunk
blatant as you like, in the high street
In the middle of the day.

And my father, his sense of humour still
intact started shouting. Help! Somebody
help me! The fucker's stealing me money!
Help! Call the police! Help me!

Billy the Kid

For Bill Hicks 1961-1994

He shot us all down.
Bullets in our belly-laughs.
Revolved us through the smoking
Barrel of his life and took no prisoners
That Billy the Kid.

No high horse for him.
His lip was hip and he let us have it
Curled and bared, he never was scared
That Billy the Kid.

Wearing black like he knew
He was going to get it any day.
Only the good die young they say.
Well I never once saw that guy die
That Billy the Kid.

Celebrity

The net of fate
has spread the cast

and the stars are
all out there

light years away
from reality

shining bright
and dead.

Sick Poem

for Adrian Mitchell

('My songs may be childish as paper planes but they glide so thanks a lot' – his response to a critic who claimed that his poems were as childish as paper planes.)

A poem, stretched to its limits
Lay dying
It was as white as a sheet
No one knew what to do

Everybody gathered around
And stared
But not one person offered a word of comfort
Not one

At that precise moment
A child just happened
To be passing
I am still on duty, the child said

I will do what I can.
Picking up the poem, the child scanned it
Very carefully
Then folded it neatly into an aeroplane

And sent it off soaring
Into flight
Shouting
There, there, that poem's all right.

Shoulder Bit

The shoulder bit that I dragged from the sodden
undergrowth of a Holly tree was a wet, hard Sycamore,
and it slipped away from me. Its bark covered in green
slime, I could see my finger marks, failure.

Exuberant, inside the noise of a plastic anorak,
sweating, steaming, in the quiet veiled rain, I sat on a
cold stone and thought for a split second, about my
Grandmother and piles. The wood was around and in me.

I knew that everything was here. Every colour and smell
and enemy and strength and weakness and love and death
and life and all the secrets. Every root to the sky and
the earth.

This was where the clean shirts and socks and shoes of
the mummy's boys came to fear. Once upon a time, deep,
in the dark, dark forest. This was where it all started,
and finished.

I stared at the long slim Sycamore. Imagined it in
neatly cut blocks, stacked up and dried out by the side
of a gable like big cigarette ends waiting for the
clear blue woodsmoke, that was freedom.

I went at it, heard it suck at the mud as it came free,
a born again tree, torn limb from limb. It was mine and
I hauled it up the hill through foliage and barbed
branches that tore at my legs and bled them.

Exhausted, I lay on top of it and felt its power.
I counted the rings, twelve, same age as me. I'll have
you! An hour later I threw it from my shoulder, a little
body wracked with pain, and bursting with pride.

All the Family cheered as it thudded and slithered on
the concrete like a frozen snake. My Grandfather was
drunk and said it would take ten years to dry out. My
Mother elbowed him and said he would take twenty.

Aunt Jeannie said it was bad luck to cut down a Sycamore
because they were graveyard trees and their branches were
the arms of the dead on All Souls Night. My brother said
it would burn like an iron bar. But my Father knew.

He smiled and shouted 'Good man yourself! You're a tight
man' He knew that his coffin would be safe on my
shoulder. That when the time came, I wouldn't let him
down. I would be well able to do my bit. My shoulder bit.

Off My Face 1

Extract from the award-winning one-man play
'Off My Face' (Edinburgh 1997)

OWEN: Everybody had gone to bed except my Dad and uncle Harry the Cockney. They were drunk and arguing loudly. I was listening from the top of the stairs.

HARRY: One chicken and ten fucking kids? What's that then? You're having a fucking laff! I mean what kind of a Christmas dinner is that going to be? One sparrow-chested chicken and ten kids? It's not mathematically possible! What are you gonna do abaht it?

DAD: We're going to have cheese as well!

HARRY: Cheese! What the fuck are you on abaht? You can't have cheese, that's shit! How can you celebrate Jesus's birfday with one chicken and a bit of cheese.

DAD: It's quite a substantial bit of cheese. . . twelve pound of cheese I think.

HARRY: That's it! I've heard enough!

HARRY LEAPS UP.

DAD: Where are you going?

HARRY: I'm going out to get something for the Christmas dinner!

DAD: (LAUGHING) Oh right enough! Good luck now. You shouldn't have any problem it's only three o'clock on Christmas morning – all the shops are open!

HARRY GOES OUT. LIGHTING CHANGE. BLUE WASH MOONLIGHT: HARRY IS FALLING THROUGH THE SNOW. HE STOPS.

HARRY: Sheepy sheepy sheepy! Come on little sheepy.

SOUND CUE: BLEATING SHEEP.

HARRY: Come on don't be shy. . . it's only your uncle Arry here.

HARRY DIVES ON THE SHEEP AND MISSES. SOUND CUE: SHEEP BLEATING.

HARRY: Stand still you woolly bastards!

HARRY CIRCLES THE SHEEP SLOWLY.

HARRY: That's it. . . come on. . . there's a good little sheepy.

HARRY DIVES ON THE SHEEP AND RIDES IT AROUND THE STAGE, HANDS FIRMLY AROUND ITS THROAT. IT THROWS HIM OFF. SOUND CUE OF SHEEP BAAAAING IN DISTRESS. HARRY HANGS ON STRANGLING THE SHEEP. SILENCE: AFTER A MOMENT HE PICKS UP THE SHEEP, THROWS IT ACROSS HIS SHOULDERS AND CARRIES IT AWAY. MUSIC CUE: THE HYMN 'APRIL LAMBS'.

OWEN: Harry came back with the sheep and threw it across the sink and when my Dad saw it. . . it was like he'd seen a ghost.

DAD: (mortified) It's a sheep!. . . it's a fuckin sheep! Is it dead?

HARRY: Course it's fucking dead. It's for the Christmas dinner!

DAD: Christmas din. . . Who the fuck eats sheep at Christmas?

HARRY: People with one chicken and ten kids!

DAD: Get it out of here! Get it to fuck out of here! Where did you get it?

HARRY: There's loads of em in the fields.

DAD: Jesus Christ!. . . You went into the field. . . and. . . killed . . . show me your hands.

HARRY HOLDS UP HIS BLOODY HANDS.

DAD: You strangled it. . . oh for fuck's sake. You're sick. . . you're a sick man.

HARRY: What do you mean sick? Look I didn't shag it. I killed it to eat. I did it for you and your kids to celebrate Jesus's birfday with a good big meal.

DAD: Do you think that's what Jesus would have wanted. . . eh? Can you imagine the little baby Jesus in the manger with all the animals crowded around blowing their breath on him to keep him warm. The ox and the donkey and the cow and then the sheep comes in to help out. . . and you leap out of the shadows and strangle the fucking thing! Have you any idea how out of place and upsetting that would've been for the Holy Family!

HARRY: Bollocks! They slaughtered sheep in those days all the time.

PAUSE AS DAD WALKS AROUND STARING AT HARRY.

DAD: You're just a sick, sheep-murdering bastard and that's the end of it.

HARRY: Read your Bible mate. Every other fucking page. . . it's 'and God said onto him go out and slaughter a lamb and while you're there you might as well kill your son

Abraham and do it for the Lord'.

DAD: Well you can tell that to big Joe McGloughlin and his brothers. They're the farmers that own that sheep. You tell them when they come looking for it that you killed it for the Lord and that I had fuck all to do with it.

OWEN: Harry eventually fell asleep mumbling about how he used to be a butcher and in the morning he would shear the sheep, bleed it and chop it up and what a feast we were all going to have. My father had other ideas. I was pretending to be asleep when he woke me and my younger brother Tommy at five am.

DAD: (LOUD WHISPER) Come on you two wake up! Wake up lads! I've something I want you to do for me.

TOMMY: (LOUDLY) Has Santa come yet!

DAD: Shooosh! You'll waken the house! Santa Claus isn't here yet. He always does us last, now get dressed hurry up!

OWEN: As we passed through the front room to the kitchen we saw Harry lying on the couch snoring. His shirt and hands covered in blood and Tommy said. . .

TOMMY: Da uncle Harry's nose is bleeding, Da uncle Harry's nose is bleeding, Da uncle Harry's nose is bleeding. . .

DAD: (CUTTING IN SHOUTING) Shut up! Your uncle Harry killed a sheep!. . . In his car. . . he hit it and it flew through the windscreen onto his lap.

TOMMY: Is he dead?

DAD: No but the sheep is! Now listen to me carefully. I want you to put the sheep in the wheelbarrow. Wheel it down to the stone bridge and throw it into the river. Because if the police find out that your uncle Harry was drinking and driving and killing sheep he'll go to prison.

OWEN: So my father puts the sheep into the wheelbarrow. The wheelbarrow is too small and the sheep's head is lolling over the side and every time we try and push it the sheep falls out. My father's hangover is beginning to descend and he's losing patience.

DAD: Can you not push a fuckin dead sheep in a wheelbarrow. What is the matter with you two for fuck's sake give me that wheelbarrow. . . watch and learn!

OWEN: It's an image that will stay with me forever. My father in his vest and socks wheeling a dead sheep in a wheelbarrow through the snow and looking manically pleased with himself, shouting. . . 'You see! That's how you do it.' But we couldn't do it. Every time we tried, the sheep fell out into the snow and was getting wetter and heavier. Then my father had an idea.

DAD: I know, I'll put it in that old supermarket trolley that's lying in the hedge.

OWEN: Thinking back on it I must have had a very warped black sense of humour. While my father was busy pulling the trolley from the hedge I sneaked into the girls' bedroom. My sister had a teddy bear and when you turned it upside down it went Baaah! and the thing that made it go Baaah! had fallen out. So I took it and put it in my pocket.

OWEN: And off we went, my little seven year old brother and I. Six o'clock on Christmas morning wheeling a dead sheep through the snow in a supermarket trolley. And then I suddenly stopped and stared at the sheep.

TOMMY: (SCARED) What?

OWEN: I think it's still alive. I saw it's foot twitching. Come on!

PAUSE.

OWEN: I raced through the snow with Tommy hanging on for dear life. Then I made the Baaah sound in my pocket BAAAAH! 'Oh Tommy the fucking thing is still alive!'

TOMMY: (SCREECHING) Ahhhhh I wanna go home!

OWEN: Keep running! There's nothing as dangerous as a half

dead sheep. If it wakes up it will fucking kill us both! BAAAAAAH!

TOMMY SCREAMING AND CRYING.

OWEN: And we plummeted down the hill slithering and falling and laughing and crying but never letting go of the trolley and the dead sheep until we finally came to rest at the bottom beside the little stone bridge. Grazed and snowy wet with the steam rising off us in the black frosty morning air. Tommy was breathing hard and the eyes on him standing out like Gobstoppers, terrified to talk in case he woke the sheep. Slowly and silently we began the onerous task of getting the sheep out of the trolley. We struggled for ten minutes. The sheep's wool had become entangled in the wire mesh. Half an hour later we managed to drag and heave it on to the wall of the bridge and push it over the side. We waited for the splash, but it never came. What we heard was a dull thud as the sheep landed on the frozen river and slid silently upstream. After a moment's silence I stood behind my brother and went BAAAAAAH! And we both ran for our lives.

PAUSE.

OWEN: When we got back home my mother was putting presents under the Christmas tree and my father was hosing the remains of the sheep's blood off the kitchen walls and Tommy started to cry, because he realised that Santa didn't exist.

CROSSFADE TO OWEN AT TABLE.

OWEN: By eight o'clock that morning all the adults in the house were suffering from severe hangovers. Harry was wearing one of my father's shirts, his was drying on the clothes line above the open fire, but you could still the pink tinges where the blood had been. He was quiet and sipped at a bottle of something. Occasionally my father would reach into a cupboard, fill a tumbler, knock it back then cough and splutter everywhere. My mother had wine in her handbag. My three aunts appeared like the Macbeth witches. They had brandy in their tea. It was like watching people arise from the dead. The drink had drained the life out of them and this topping up ceremony was like a kind of ressurection before another descent into the inevitable merry hell.

PAUSE

OWEN: On the way to eleven o'clock mass all the family trooped over the little stone bridge across the Ballinderry river. The adults now half pissed. Suddenly everyone stopped in the middle and looked down. . . and there, lying on its back, frozen stiff, with all its four legs in the air, was the sheep. . . and Harry said, 'That'll never be defrosted by the time we get home.'

Ah Come On

Ah come on; let me tell you how much I love you.
Let me tell you that I don't mind when you write
Weird things on the shopping list, things like 'something different'.
Come on; let me show you how much I love you.

Ah come on; let me tell you how much I love you. I'm sorry
That I said Joanna Lumley was looking great for her age and not
An ounce of fat on her, I'm sorry I said that, two years ago.
Come on; let me show you how much I love you.

Ah come on; let me tell you how much I love you. I don't mind
That when I asked you who you fantasised about when I was
Making love to you and you said you didn't have time.
Come on; let me show you how much I love you.

Ah come on; let me tell you how much I love you.
I'm sorry that I teased you in front of your boss
When you said place-bo in stead of pla-cebo.
Come on; let me show you how much I love you.

Ah come now; let me tell you how much I love you.
Look she was my cousin. . . nothing happened, really, she
Had nowhere else to go, I thought her name was Lucy
Lucy, Becky, what does it matter? I hadn't seen her in a while.

Ah come on Jesus put the knife down. . . that's stupid.
Let me tell you how much I love you. Come on! Wow!
That was fucking close! Now put the knife down. . . come on
Let me tell you how muchhhhhhhh aggggggggh shittttttttttt!!!

The Meaning of Life. . . Almost

Words like slither, sweat, slippery, blood soaked,
umbilical cord, push, push, pant, pant or fuck off
this is all your fault you bastard! never occurred
during the birth of our son.

Instead, it seemed that, while his Mother was
frowning, struggling to remember something
important and I was hovering reading a poem called
The Cuckoo

He sort of slow motioned himself backwards out from
between her thighs looking like he was about to
sneeze. It was as if he had been there all of our
lives, waiting.

Waiting, I felt I owed him an apology. So I said
sorry we kept you hanging about, we just didn't get
around to it, sorry. Then suddenly I instinctively
knew that he had come a long way,

From some ancient civilisation and that he knew
the real meaning of life because he was so close to
it. I wanted to ask him what it was like, where he
had come from, what he wanted and what was my role in it all.

I knew I didn't have much time and that I had to
work fast and concentrate but people kept getting
in the way. And then he filled up his lungs and
when he opened his mouth, it wasn't a cry.

No one could call it a cry. It was a song! It took over everything, it filled up every gap inside of me until I was bursting. And then I realised he too wanted to communicate. With his great wonderous, sonorous, sonic song. Yes! Yes! I shouted. Yes! And I joined in.

Waaaaaaahhhhhhhhhhhhhhhhhhhhhhhhhhhhhhhhhhhh
hhhhhhhhhhhhhhhhhhhhhhhhhhhhhhhhhhhhhhhhhhhhhhhhh!

And just as I was about to know the answer, two men in white coats carried me into the corridor.

Omagh. Ten Past Three.

The clocks did stop.
In a moment, in that market place
and a child upon her father's shoulders
saw the World upon a rock.

The Sperrin mountains, in the distance
solid as time itself
could do nothing
but sit, and wait.

In that sheer second of cut glass.
Their very own trusted bricks
laid safe and straight as a die
sharp edged and lethal now

hardened in the kiln. Killing.
Sending home the message, that no one
wanted to hear. Innocence, savaged and
deadly strewn in that market place.

The clocks did stop.
There will always be children
upon their father's shoulders
seeing the World upon a rock.

The Sperrin mountains, in the distance
solid as time itself
will do nothing
but sit and wait.

And I
can also do nothing
but sit, and wait
for the clocks to start.

Off My Face 2

OWEN: There were three clothes shops in our town owned by Mr Andy Wilson, Freemason and Master of the local Orange lodge. My uncle Harry robbed all three of his shops in one night and I was his accomplice. Harry was Spiderman. He could climb up anything. He needed me because all three shops had skylights. I was light and skinny and could be lowered through when the skylight was smashed. I'll never forget just hanging there until my eyes became accustomed to the dark.

HARRY: Can you see anyfink yet?

OWEN: No. Give it a minute.

HARRY: Come on we can't hang around here all night.

OWEN: Okay if you can swing me left a bit and then drop me I won't land on the counter.

HARRY: Fuck's sake. Trapeze artists we are. Should be in a circus.

OWEN: So Harry swung me to the left and then let go and I dropped some eight feet on to the shop floor missing the counter by a few inches. I opened the side door and Harry was in. He knew where everything was and exactly what he wanted. . . 'cor look at that, your mum'll love that. . . oooh nice bit of suede and look at those suits and Ben Sherman shirts. Tasty'. It took us less than thirty minutes to stuff forty industrial bin bags full of clothes. The transit van was crammed to the front window.

PAUSE.

OWEN: When my father saw the bags of clothes scattered around our back yard he almost had a fit.

DAD: Oh for Jesus sake Harry, the quicker you fuck off back to London the better. What do you think you're playing at? You've got to get rid of these. You've got to dump them.

HARRY: What do you mean dump them? They're new clothes for your ten kids and your Missus!

DAD: My kids and missus don't wear new clothes. If the police see us in new clothes they'll arrest the fucking lot of us!

HARRY: Come on relax. I also did the off-licence on the way home.

OWEN: Harry then produced two large bottles of Black Bush whiskey.

HARRY: Come on have a snort.

OWEN: My dad protested and moaned and groaned but as the whiskey went down he became less and less concerned about the clothes.

TWO HOURS LATER.

DAD: Harry. . . you're a fuckin decent man you know that. . . a decent man. How many suits did you get me?

HARRY: Fifteen.

DAD: Fifteen!. . . Fifteen fuckin suits! I'll go to every funeral in the country!. . . Did you get me any socks?

HARRY: Yeah.

DAD: How many socks did you get me?

HARRY: A thousand.

DAD: A thousand!. . . Fuck off! There's no such thing as a thousand socks. . . a thousand socks. . . Jesus. I'm going to go down to Andy Wilson's drapers shop in the morning and I'm going to say. . . Good Morning Andy. You fuckin baldy Orange cunt! Do you know how many socks I have Andy?. . . One thousand! So go and fuck yourself!

OWEN: And then Harry and my dad almost killed themselves laughing. But of course the next day was a different story. The whiskey was gone, so was Harry and my Fathers's fear was back with a vengeance. The robbery had made the headlines in the local paper. WILSON'S SUFFER TRIPLE ROBBERY. DARING GANG RAID ON DRAPERS SHOP.

PAUSE.

OWEN: My father was so frightened of being caught he decided to take drastic action. We had an enormous tin trunk that my grandad had brought back from the war, a huge thing. My father crammed it full with all the clothes, dug a six foot grave and buried it in the back garden. . . but of course; he'd get drunk again come back to the house with a few of his drinking pals and his mind would start thinking about money for the next day's drinking.

DAD: Hey Jimmy. . . do you want to buy a suit? Brand new and I'll throw in a pair of shoes and four socks. Fifteen quid the lot!

OWEN: Well, soon everybody was clamouring for orders.

DAD: OK OK keep your hair on there's plenty for everybody. So that's three suits, chests 38 42 40, four pair of shoes size 9 and sixteen socks. Owen! Go get the spade.

OWEN: We had our own boutique in the back garden.

Poem for Margaret

I am sitting here watching her.
Watching her sisters and husband
and daughters and son, busy themselves
with the making of tea and the buttering
of bread.

Every minute detail is attended to with
great purpose and the talk is so small
it disappears into the corners and hangs
there enormous.

Behind the gasping yellowed illness
which has turned her old, I see the
old her, and she has the time to
register my grief.

Patting the bed softly she tells me to
sit. I sit, take her bruised hand in mine
and she leans in and hugs me, and all I
can do is sob and say sorry, I'm sorry.

She tells me it's all right, but everything
has deserted me, all the tricks I've
learned, all the restraint, all the holding
back, the keeping it together, all that is gone.

I'm comforted here by my dying sister and
it's all right she says, it's all right. Before
I leave, I kiss her on the forehead. She opens
her eyes, smiles and gives me the thumbs up.

I walk outside into the sunshine and I'm
so proud of her. I want to tell everyone.
I want to say, come and see, come and see my
sister, come and see how it's done.

Schoolbag

It was the first leather thing I can remember
all big buckles and resilient hard newness
with brass rivets and stitching and everything
fitting into itself with nothing left to spare
shiny on the outside and dull on the inside
like a brown horse's ear.

My schoolbag was too big for me, knocking
at my shins, the two of us full of emptiness
on our first day, but coming home proud at
three o'clock with Janet and John and a jotter.
I was soon to grow into it, learn to love it. It
would become my protector, weighed down

with the hard spines of Joyce and Hardy and
Steinbeck whirling through the air at my enemies
a windmill of lethal knowledge that would bust
your head wide open. It was a goalpost when a
spontaneous game of football would last into the
dark days of an echoey winter

and all we were really left kicking was a piece of
freedom away from home and work, even in that
country blackness I knew it was mine, picking it
out immediately from all the others like a blind
man feeling a face. I learned to wear it well, broke
it down like a bucking bronco until it buckled more

easily and lay gently on my side. Forty years on
and the smell of leather, no matter what it is, is
always my schoolbag, sour hawthorn black ink
woody pencil shavings, rubbers tired of rubbing
and the crumbs of stale bread and education. It was
all the real learning I ever had, inside that bag.

They are vanishing now, leather schoolbags.
Cyberspace and screens are the future, easily
carried and soon forgotten. I saw one the other day
in a junk shop, circa 1960. I bought it, clutched
it to my heart, and some day when I'm very old
and disappeared, they will find me, wandering in
my pyjamas, on the hard shoulder, swinging my
schoolbag, ready for a fight.

New York

Walk! Don't walk!
Walk!
Don't walk!
Walk!
Don't walk!
Walk!
Don't walk!
Walk!
Don't walk!
Walk!
Don't walk!
Walk!
Don't walk!
Walk!
Don't walk!
Walk!
Don't fuckin walk!
Fuck you!
I'm walking here!

The Snip

for Janet Dick

A snip they call it. A snip?
A snip that will pass in the night.
Listen, a snip is something half-arsed.
Roses get snipped by perfumed ladies.
Just a snip Mr. Hairdresser please
that's all I need.

A snip is over in seconds.
A wee small thing is a snip.
Sure it's only a snip.
Well listen here you bunch of Hoors!
you can go and suck your secateurs
because I'll give you a snip.

It was a great bastard swathe that a sword
would take centuries to hack through.
Men in boats came to stare at it.
Vikings blew their horns in despair at it
and slaves wept at the sight of its thickness
and power.

We will never get through that they screamed!
Somebody chop the bastard down before it kills
us all. Pull it! Push it! Punch it! Whip it!
Kick it! Stab it! Fuckin grab it! Jesus Christ
in his mercy. Somebody! Stop it before it does
anymore damage.

Then the slight red headed woman walked out
from the raging sea. Held up her hands and
said quietly. . . all right, all right! What's all
the fuss about? I'll see to it. And all the
men went back to sleep to suck their thumbs
and clutch their balls.

Somewhere in Janet's house there is a vase
with something growing in it. Something that
will bloom and make her happy. She said it
was just the perfect size and had all the
right colours. I bought it for her after the
operation. . .

it wasn't a snip.

It Was Henry Fonda's Fault

Extract from It was Henry Fonda's Fault (Edinburgh, 2001)

OWEN IS FOURTEEN YEARS OLD AND IS INSPIRED BY JAZZ HEGARTY, THE TORCH-MAN AND FORMER HOLLYWOOD STUNT-MAN WHO NOW RUNS THE LOCAL FLEA-PIT CINEMA.

JAZZ IS BEING JEERED AND LAUGHED AT BY THE YOUNG SATURDAY MORNING AUDIENCE.

JAZZ: Right come on out! I don't care what it says on the poster outside! This is my Picture House and I'll show what I like! Out! Do you think that Henry Fonda spent weeks learning his lines so as you bunch of inbreds could sit there pulling chewing gum out of your faces and laughing and kehoeing like lunatics? Do you think that I risked my life falling off horses and down stairs and out of windows only to be laughed at by the scum of this place! What are youse doing here?

That's what I'd like to know. For you're not in the least bit interested in giving Henry Fonda a chance. You're not in the least bit interested in anything except ripping the seats with knives, crackling sweetie papers, putting your hands down each others pants and sucking the gobs off one another, that's what you're here for! Don't think I don't know what you're all up to.

JAZZ TAKES A BREATHER.

JAZZ: You wouldn't do it in a church would you? Well this is a church. . . this is my church and do you see that light up there! That's the light that illuminates the darkness . . . that's the light that brings joy and hope and laughter and wisdom to the humdrum existence of millions and millions of people. . . more people look up to that light than look up to Jesus Christ himself!. . . and I'll tell you something else; it never lets them down. Dreams come true up there. . . so don't you ever come back to this picture house until you can give it some respect. . . now clear off!

JAZZ: Go on. Get out!

JAZZ: Not you young O'Neill. You hang on there son for I know you were watching and you were moved by what you saw. I know you were because you stopped chewing your chewing gum.

JAZZ SITS BESIDE OWEN.

JAZZ: Me and you will watch it on our own son. It'll be a lot quieter with those reprobates out of the way. This film is called the Grapes of Wrath. One of Henry Fonda's greatest.

PAUSE.

JAZZ: A star. That's what he was, a real star and a gentleman. The Grapes of Wrath is one of his greatest performances. He was only a young man then. . . and so was I. . . California was some place in those days. . . Hollywood! What a town. I met them all you know. . . Gary Cooper . . . Coop they used to call him. Jimmy Stewart, Jimmy Cagney, Randolph Scott, Henry Fonda. . . Hank he liked to be called. . . all gentlemen everyone of them. I was a stunt man for them all but mostly for Hank because we were about the same size, apart from his hands. . . he had the tiniest hands, woman's hands, like a wee bunch of newborn pink mice. And the Director John Ford, was always telling me to keep my big hands up my sleeves or make a fist of them you know. . . wee hands. . . I could go anywhere in Hollywood in those days. Everybody knew Jazz Hegarty. I drove a Coupe de Ville, had money in the bank and the telephone numbers of over 200 women in my wallet. . . swell times. . .

OWEN: I'd love to be in the fillums Jazz. Do you think I could?

JAZZ: Of course you could! I did. Go to Hollywood son. Follow your dreams. Don't be scared! Dreams are what the future is made of.

TWENTY YEARS LATER, STILL INSPIRED BY JAZZ, OWEN IS PERSUADED BY JERRY, AN AMERICAN FAN, TO TAKE HIS ONE MAN PLAY 'OFF MY FACE' TO HOLLYWOOD. JERRY IS NOT AT L.A. AIRPORT TO PICK OWEN UP LIKE HE PROMISED. OWEN GETS A CAB AND WAITS OUTSIDE HIS APARTMENT.

JERRY: Owen. . . . please forgive me, I am so sorry. I am such a lousy host. I was at an AA meeting, my head was just not right today so my Higher Power said to me 'Jerry, get to a meeting.' So I did because my life is in his hands right now. You been here long?

OWEN: Three hours.

PAUSE.

OWEN: Jerry showed me around his apartment. It was a shrine to AA. Then he took me into the kitchen and that's when things got very spooky. On the back wall, above the fridge, there were twelve pictures. . . of me. Stills from when I did the show in Edinburgh. And he could pin-point the very scene where he realised he was an alcoholic. 'There,' he said, pointing to one of the photos, 'that one, when you were strangling the sheep on Christmas Eve; that was the moment. I owe my life to you Owen.'

PAUSE.

OWEN: The Hudson Citadel Theatre where I was performing was on Santa Monica Boulevard. In my imagination Santa Monica Boulevard was a little road lined with palm trees and nice restaurants. . . it's not. Santa Monica Boulevard is a twenty-five mile long dual carriageway full of horrible flat roofed concrete buildings and cheap shops.

PAUSE.

OWEN: I got a real shock when I got to the theatre. The Hudson Backstage wasn't even on Santa Monica Boulevard. It was behind the main Hudson Citadel Theatre in a dead-end street beside a scrap yard that had a car crushing plant. I hammered on a big black door for ten minutes. . . nothing. I went around to the main theatre and asked had anybody seen Valerie – no one had seen her.

PAUSE.

OWEN: Valerie eventually turned up. Two hours late. . . and she was bonkers. She was about twenty stone and completely bald. She had three eyebrow rings in each eyebrow, a leopard skin top with rips in it and her flesh was protruding from the rips like bunches of pork sausages! She was wearing a very tight pair of red PVC trousers and black cowboy boots with silver spurs. She did not suit any of these clothes because the woman was at least fifty years old and grossly overweight. When she moved, her trousers squeaked.

OWEN WALKS ACROSS THE STAGE AND DOES THE SQUEAK.

OWEN: I kept thinking her pager was going off.

VALERIE: Owen. We meet at last! Your hair is so red. I recognise you from the flyers you sent. Have you seen the space?

OWEN: No. There was no one here to let me in. We were supposed to meet at one o'clock.

VALERIE: One o'clock?

OWEN: And she takes out a personal organiser.

VALERIE: Three o'clock honey. . . this is never wrong. Come through I'll show you the space and introduce you to Lisabelle who will be your technician and if I could have the other fourteen hundred dollars that would be great the banks close in half an hour.

OWEN: Valerie took me through a maze of little corridors and walkways. There were no windows in the place and everything was in pitch darkness. I couldn't see a thing I just followed the squeak in front of me. All the time she's shouting. Lisabelle! It's Valerie. Owen O'Neill is here. Lisabelle?

VALERIE: Lisabelle!

OWEN: I could hear this strange noise. . . like Vooozzze! Vooozzze! Voooozzzze! The lights came on and when I saw the space where I would be performing for the next ten nights. . . my heart sank. . . I couldn't believe it. . . and I'm trying to take everything in and remain calm. . . maybe this wasn't the place. . . Valerie had made a mistake and took me into a disused toilet.

VALERIE: Well here we are. This is it.

OWEN: She hadn't.

PAUSE.

OWEN: The stage was the first disaster, it was tiny, about eight foot square and there was no wings to get off and on. Just a brick wall at the back, no door, and two brick walls down the side. The wall at the back was painted white and had a rainbow across it and on the stage itself was a park bench screwed to the floor. To get off the stage you literally had to walk off the stage into the audience and through the exit door. It was just a brick box and I looked up at the lighting rig and there were only two lights, one on each corner and that noise Vooozzze Vooozzze Voooozzzze! . . . which turned out to be Lisabelle. . . asleep in the back row. Vooozzze Vooozzze.

VALERIE: Lisabelle? Is that you? Lisabelle!

LISABELLE: Vooozzze vooozzze. . . Huh. . . uh Hi Valerie. I'm sorry I must have dozed off.

VALERIE: Oh my god have you had a relapse? Lisabelle?

LISABELLE: Noooo. How could you think that. . . I just fell asleep it's hot in here.

VALERIE: Owen meet Lisabelle your technician. She's very good, if not a little tired.

OWEN: Lisabelle was six feet tall with hunched shoulders, a thin face and long lank greasy hair plastered to her forehead

LISABELLE: I haven't had my medication. So I have to take it right now.

VALERIE: OK. You have your break, take your medication and be back by four o'clock.

PAUSE.

VALERIE: Owen don't look so shocked. Lisabelle is just a recovering heroin addict. She's on methadone right now. She's what's known as a C.S. community server. She has to sign on with the LAPD every morning, but she's doing fine and she's a very competent technician. So don't worry! Are you excited about being in LA?

OWEN: In the contract it says that the Hudson Backstage is a fully operational theatre am I right? Is that what it said? . . . Is that what it said?

VALERIE: Yes! That's what it said and it is a full. . .

OWEN: Where? Where is this fully operational theatre? Where the fuck is it?

VALERIE: How dare you talk to me like that? Who the hell do you think you are?

OWEN: What you've rented me is a brick shit house with two bulbs for a lighting rig and a narcoleptic heroin addict for a technician!

VALERIE: You are so gross!

OWEN: I cannot do my show in this space!

VALERIE: (CUTTING IN) You will not be doing your show anywhere until you pay me fourteen hundred dollars.

OWEN: Fuck you! And your fourteen hundred dollars! I open here tomorrow night and if that rainbow mural isn't gone from there! If that park bench isn't removed and if I haven't got a proper lighting rig and follow spot and WINGS! I want all my money back!

MUSIC CUE 'NO BUSINESS LIKE SHOW BUSINESS'. OWEN DOES THE CAN-CAN.

OWEN: I was so depressed. Everything was going wrong. Hollywood wasn't supposed to be like this.

OWEN: Later on that night I got a call from Valerie.

VALERIE: Hi Owen Valerie here. I read your script last night. Now, I have had a word with the show that goes up before you and when they finish they are happy to put a dark cloth over the rainbow and remove their park bench. I have a lighting rig coming in the morning and will hire a follow spot. I've made two hinged flats for you that will act as wings. I'm sorry we got off on the wrong foot. I will need you to bring the rest of the deposit with you tomorrow. . . please, otherwise no show. Bye now.

OWEN: That made me feel a lot better. In the morning I'd get up really early, go out on the streets of L.A. and start leafleting!

SOUND CUE: SPEEDING TRAFFIC/CAR HORNS ETC. OWEN STANDS ON STAGE TRYING TO LEAFLET PASSING CARS.

OWEN: It's impossible to leaflet on the streets because there's nobody on the streets in LA apart from drunks, lunatics, and people running to their cars. I got on a bus and went all the way to Santa Monica beach, it took an hour and a half but it was worth it because when I got there everybody took a leaflet . . . oh wow is this you inside the bottle? Oh we'll definitely come and see your show. We're not doing anything tonight, sure we'll be there, sounds great. I handed out three thousand leaflets.

MUSIC CUE: NEIL DIAMOND 'L.A.'S FINE'.

OWEN: These are the wings that Valerie has provided which has now reduced the stage to five feet square. The show starts in two hours and the tech run-through with Lisabelle is not going well.

PAUSE.

OWEN: OK Lisabelle let's try it one more time.

LISABELLE: It would be much better if you didn't raise your voice to me.

OWEN: OK Lisabelle I'll try not to. . . but we've been here two hours and we're still on the first scene. . . so let's try and concentrate and get it right. OK we go from pre-set to blackout. Then we have music cue number one which is Lilac Wine, which you play in blackout. I walk from behind the flat and then you bring up the spotlight and fade the music. I do my dialogue then I walk away. You fade the spotlight and go straight into music cue number two which is Motorhead, Ace of Spades. OK?

LISABELLE: OK. . . I got it. . . yeh. . .

OWEN: Lose the lights.

LIGHTS GO TO BLACKOUT.

MUSIC CUE: 'LILAC WINE '

OWEN: No Lisabelle. . . please listen. You do not bring up the spotlight until I hit my mark on the stage.

LISABELLE: OK sorry. . . I hit the wrong button. . . sorry.

OWEN: From the top.

PAUSE.

OWEN: Lose the lights.

OWEN GOES BEHIND THE FLAT. IT GOES TO BLACKOUT. MUSIC CUE; 'LILAC WINE' COMES ON REALLY LOW. OWEN COMES OUT.

OWEN: Lisabelle! It's too low! I can't hear it.

LISABELLE: Sor-reee. . . sorry. I nudged the lever. Sorry.

OWEN: OK from the top.

OWEN GOES BEHIND THE FLAT. WE ARE STILL IN BLACKOUT FOR A LONG TIME, ABOUT EIGHT SECONDS.

OWEN: What's the prob. . . .

MUSIC CUE. A VERY LOUD BLAST OF 'ACE OF SPADES' FROM MOTORHEAD.

OWEN DOES HIS NUT.

OWEN: Turn it down! Turn the fucking thing down! You stupid fucking dopey heroin fuckhead!

LISABELLE: (STARTS TO WIMPER) That's really unfair. . . You have no right to call me that. . . I'm really trying. It's hard for me. . . up here on my own. . . I'm trying to fight this illness.

OWEN: I'm sorry. . . I'm sorry I called you a heroin fuckhead. I know it's hard. . . but I open in under two hours. . . you can't do this Lisabelle. You haven't got a clue. It's not your fault. I'm going to have to phone Valerie and get someone else.

LISABELLE: (STARTS TO WAIL) No please. . . just give me another chance. I promise I'll try really really hard. If I lose this job I'll have to go back to rehab! Just give me another chance. . . pleassssse!

OWEN: An hour and a half later we had only gotten through Scene Two. Tomorrow I would see Valerie and demand a new techie. As for tonight. . . well I just had to pray.

PAUSE.

OWEN: The show started at nine thirty. It was now nine fifteen . . . well there could be a late rush. . . people were always late. . . nine thirty five. . . nobody. . . ten to ten . . . nothing. . . at ten o'clock Lisabelle came down from the sound box and said:

LISABELLE: If nobody comes do you still want to do the run through. . . like for practice. . . I don't mind.

OWEN: I was just about to tell her to piss off and die when I heard this loud screeching noise of metal being ripped apart.

SOUND CUE: RIPPING METAL.

OWEN: I thought it was a car crash so I ran outside to have a look. . . It was the scrap yard across from the theatre, they started their car-crunching night shift at ten o'clock . . . something else Valerie forgot to mention.

PAUSE.

OWEN: Nobody came on the opening night. I couldn't face going home so I kept Lisabelle there until she got it right. Twelve fifteen we finished. It had taken her fourteen hours to tech my show. The next morning Jerry asked me how the show went. I told him it was sold out and I got a standing ovation.

PAUSE.

OWEN: No one came on the second night.

PAUSE.

OWEN: No one came on the third night, or the fourth night, or on the fifth or sixth nights, on the sixth night Jerry said he was coming with a few of his mates from AA. I told him I was sold out. He said he would pray to his higher power for a couple of tickets.

PAUSE.

OWEN: No one came on the seventh night. On the eighth night even the box office staff didn't turn up. I sat in that theatre on my own listening to Lisabelle snoring in the back row. . . vooozzze vooozzze. . . and the sound of cars being crushed across the road in the scrap yard. Oh yeah. Money well spent.

SOUND CUE: METAL RIPPING.

OWEN: On the ninth night no one came. I had flown three thousand miles, was nearly ten thousand dollars out of pocket! And I hadn't even performed my show once! I had given out three thousand leaflets! Three thousand! How could three thousand people bullshit you ? I knew whose fault this was and I was going to ring him right now and tell him!

OWEN AT TABLE WITH PHONE..

OWEN: Hello! Jazz? Is that you? It's me Owen! I sound far away because I am far away! And it's your fault! You shouldn't tell children lies. Do you know that? That's the worst sin in the world. I believed you Jazz. You made me go after a dream! Which is now a fuckin nightmare! You were never a stuntman were you! You were never in Hollywood in your life! You're just a stupid pathetic old bastard with a torch and a few reels of old film that you picked up in a junk shop somewhere.

Well fuck you Jazz! I'll never speak to you again in my life! Hollywood is full of shit and so are you!

OWEN SLAMS DOWN THE PHONE.

OWEN: I needed a drink... I hadn't had a drink in five years.

PAUSE.

OWEN: When I awoke in the morning the house was deadly quiet. Either Jerry had left really early or he hadn't come home all night. To be honest at this point I really didn't care. Tonight was my last show and then I was out of this shithole forever never to return. I was going to cancel and then I thought. . . no. . . I've paid for the theatre. So I'm going to go down there and go through the motions. . . one more time.

OWEN: I got to the theatre an hour and a half before the show was due to start and I just sat at the back. . . and started thinking about how much money I'd lost. I stopped counting at twelve thousand dollars. . . and then Lisabelle came up to me and said. . .

LISABELLE: . . . Owen I want you to do something for me. I know you have had a really shit time. . . and. . . I'll understand if you don't want to. . . but I would really like to see your show. . . I've worked really hard on it. . . I'd like you to do your show for me. . . would you do that?

OWEN: And I thought why not. It's the last night. So I said sure. . . OK let's do it. It was the first time I'd ever seen Lisabelle smile.

LISABELLE: Way to go Dude!

OWEN: So I did the show and I gave quite a good performance

considering, and Lisabelle was spot on with every cue. . . I really enjoyed myself and at the end Lisabelle walked up to me and gave me a hug.

LISABELLE: (TEARFUL) Oh. . . Owen that was so sad. . . Oh my God. . .thank you.

OWEN: Afterwards I walked out of the theatre and I kept walking, and I thought I must keep walking because, if I stop walking, I'll have a drink. I walked for a long time until I found myself on Hollywood Boulevard outside the Mann Chinese theatre where the handprints of all the stars past and present are on the pavement.

BLACKOUT: OPEN SPOTLIGHT CENTRE STAGE . OWEN WALKS AROUND THE SPOT.

OWEN: John Wayne. . . Burt Lancaster. . . Whoopi Goldberg . . . Tom Cruise and Nicole Kidman together. . . Jack Lemmon. . .

OWEN: And there. . . in the corner. . . were Henry Fonda's hands. . .

OWEN DROPS TO HIS KNEES AND PUTS HIS HANDS IN THE IMPRINTS. HE BREAKS DOWN IN TEARS.

OWEN: . . .and they were. . . tiny. . . I'm sorry Jazz. . . I'm so sorry. . .

Drama in the Good Book Shop

Oh my God!

There it was, shamelessly white and long, perched
in her brown tipped fingers, smouldering.

She sucked upon it, collapsing her face. Then
talked out the smoke. Replying to the young
assistant, who looked younger.

'Well!' she shrieked, looking for a sign
'where does
it say you must not smoke?' I too, searched
desperately for a sign.

'There is none,' said the young assistant in a
strong bookish voice free from wheeze. 'Well then,'
she squawked. 'What do you expect?' And was gone
leaving the puff of smoke, wafting, unable to
defend itself.

'What a stupid old cunt' said the young assistant
spoiling the moment.

Broken

'They say a rock can split if it's hot enough.'
The stubbled man talked about this
in the bar.

She was the only woman in there. She said her
mother had died of a broken heart
but no one heard her.

'Split right down the middle. So big you could
crawl inside. It's the heat, an Aboriginal told
me. Saw it with his own eyes.'

She said her mother never opened the curtains
again. Couldn't bear to see another living thing.
The cat was mad with hunger when they found her.

'Doesn't matter how hard it is!' He was shouting
now, the beer was catching him, it was on his tail.
'In fact the harder the better!'

When they found her she was dressed in his clothes
even had his working boots on. Her tired little
feet, at peace, inside those size tens.

'They say when it cracks!. . . There's a holy terror
of a sound. . . like ripping thunder!
And then. . . and then the rain comes.'

She said it rained that day. . .
it just . . . rained. . . . and rained. . . and rained
didn't stop.

What

I felt it go

Struggle through a dream and drift away. Awake now,
not quite knowing what had gone, what I'd lost.
Empty all day.

Empty and sad without a death to blame. Wanting
something back, I kept repeating my name, over and
over. Maybe I'm insane.

The next night

I could feel it coming back, it hung around in the
darkness like an argument waiting to be settled. I
waited.

Then it spoke

'I was willing' it said in a familiar voice. 'I was
tired of being willing in weak flesh'. What do you
want me to do? I asked.

'I'm willing to give you another chance' it said.
I wasn't sure what it was that I didn't want to
lose

So I said thanks. And whatever it was. . . came back.

Volcano Dancing

He wanted to be up there
tip-toeing on the rim of the World
firewatered and full to the throat
unquenchable, no questions asked
just dancing on the volcano.

He desperately sought the heat
of the moment, a place to rage and
be forgiven, thought he was alone
while everyone watched and he
did his thing, his fool and king.

He climbed long to the top
where he finally found the bottom.
Never wanting to see the view.
Never wanted the dust to settle.
Never wanted a me and you.

He never looked for that place between
two stools, somewhere safe to fall, he just
wanted to be up there, tip-toeing on the rim
of the World, occasionally staring into hell
and then of course. . . he jumped.

Lazarus was sleeping

Lazarus was sleeping. That was it.
Dead to the World.
And Jesus of Nazareth, not to be confused
with Jesus of Jordan, entered into his room
with the whole holy circus in tow.

He laid hands on Lazarus, leaned over
and bit him on the earlobe. Lazarus
awoke with a start and the sarcasm, there
was no need for it, all that cheering and
wailing now that he was awake and walking.

Just because he liked to sleep during the day
he had a reputation as a lazy man.
I'm taking my bed with me he shouted
I'll find somewhere else to have a nap at lunchtime
away from these fucking clowns.

No one leaves cafe italia angry (If they keep their glasses on)

Heathrow. I was tired and irritable. I removed my glasses
And rubbed my eyes. A coffee, that's what I needed.
A coffee and a sit down. I put my glasses away and
bought a coffee from Starbucks. I hate Starbucks coffee.
And there was nowhere to sit.

No one leaves Cafe Italia angry.
that was their slogan, that's what it
said on their brown bags at Cafe Italia
Heathrow airport terminal 3.
The man who worked there was from Uzbekistan.

He spoke English like a Russian. 'You cannot
dreenk Starbooks coffee here! You must live now'
'I'm not going to be long' I replied. As if time
was the real problem. 'No you must live now! Only
Cafe Italia here no Starbooks'

'Look' I said 'I don't even like Starbucks' As if
Starbucks was the real problem. 'They don't have any seats'
I took a swig of the medium warm large cafe latte. 'Please
You must live now' 'Look' I said again. 'Just give me one
Of your cups and I'll pour my coffee into it.

No one will be any the wiser.' As if the container was
the real problem. 'This must be very senseless soogestion
becuz coffee steel is not from Cafe Italia! You
understand?' 'Look' I said, a third time. I'm going to New
York' As if my destination was the real problem.

'I'm tired, my bag is heavy.' I took another long drink from my nearly cold large cafe latte. 'You are deleebrately dreenking now after my request for you to stop. I do not Like thees talking to myself.' I was getting angry. Cafe Italia's slogan was obviously untrue.

'You're making me angry' I said, pointing at the slogan. 'Just let me finish my coffee, one more mouthful it's not the end of the World. Relax, take it easy, Heathrow's a stressful place.' 'Cafe Italia company pullicy only coffee purchased here can be consumed.' 'On the premises' I said quickly 'yes I know.'

'Then why you so smart man you steel break rule?' 'You should read your slogan' I said, raising my angry voice. 'On that bag over there! You tell me what it says! Go on! Read it!' He picked up the bag. 'Thees bag?' 'Yes that bag. Read your slogan.' He leaned towards me.

'I do not have to read slogan. I know what slogan say I aim manager here.' 'Well why don't you tell me then. Go on tell me what it says on your bag.' 'And then you will live?' 'Yes then I will leave.' 'It says on bag, no one Lives Cafe Italia hungry'.

I put on my glasses,
got up and
left. I was very angry.

Shoot 'em up real good

For photographer Michael Thorsnes. Bantry Bay 2010

Michael is a cowboy, has a horse underneath
him when he walks, his lens low down there
on his hip.

Michael looks at you like no one else I know.
He will find you, and *your* soul. Even Geronimo's
would be safe in his hands.

One shot between the eyes, caught forever. The
Parkinson's makes Michael speak in a low drawl
Like Clint Eastwood. 'Stand over there, look up, look down,

don't move, turn around, walk away.' You trust him,
because you know he's going to take you somewhere
beautiful.

It's in the background, he says, the colour and the shape
of things. When I look at myself through Michael's eyes
he shows me my father, my Grandmother. That turn in

the lip, that fleck of green in the eye, that's my Uncle Joe.
Yes Michael, it is in the background, the shape of things
not to be forgotten.

Down by the Sally Gardens. That's Michael's song now.
When I hear it, I will see him ride out there, silhouetted
against the sky, far out on the plain and there is a Sunset

of course there is. When I bade him farewell, we shook hands. His shake is strong and full of spirit. At the Airport, Clint Eastwood approached me and said

'Do you feel lucky today punk? Well, do you?'And I said, 'Yes Mister Eastwood, I do feel lucky today. I feel real lucky. I met Michael Thorsnes.'

Thirsty Books by Eddie Gibbons

Stations of the Heart

"A vivid human achievement...

I'm moved by the [poet's] loyalties to people and places...

Portrait of Ana Dali is one of the best British poems of recent times.

A masterpiece."

LES MURRAY

The Republic of Ted

"...It is rare for such unpretentious poetry to be so subtle and complex, and equally rare for an elegy to evoke the person and their absence so convincingly. An articulate, powerful book."

THE SCOTSMAN

Game On!

Extracts from this book were broadcast on two episodes of 'Soccer AM' on Sky Sports TV.

Eddie's latest collection, 'What They Say About You', published by Leamington Books, Edinburgh, was shortlisted for the Scottish Poetry Book of the Year, 2011.

SHORTLISTED
SALTIRE FIRST BOOK OF THE YEAR 2005

[This] collection is a breath of fresh air. The words jump off the page like wee arrows, always finding their mark. Economy is an understatement – the poems are chiselled to the bone – the apparent simplicity of the wit breathtaking, the careful structure light and unobtrusive. **Pam Besant**

These are powerfully feminist poems, in a rumbustious and confident way that we could use more of, at the moment. They are deeply rooted in the real experience of working-class women in Scotland now. They're full of anger, but also of self-knowledge, and profound compassion for the victims of violence.

Joyce McMillan

£6.99 pbk www.argyllpublishing.co.uk